from birth to
one hundred
and two

Poems by Wilma Christine Guzman

Published by Kinetics Design
kdbooks.ca   linkedin.com/in/kdbooks

ISBN 978-1-988360-07-2 (paperback)
ISBN 978-1-988360-08-9 (ePUB)
ISBN 978-1-988360-09-6 (ePDF)

Cover photograph by Wilma Christine Guzman
Angel statue from Country Garden Concrete, Erin, Ontario
Edited by David Helleman

All interior photographs by Wilma Christine Guzman
christinesmusings5@gmail.com

Cover design, and interior typesetting:
Daniel Crack, Kinetics Design, kdbooks.ca
linkedin.com/in/kdbooks

The Poems

Inspired by Nature

Home and Community Life

Life at Work

Literature and Movies

Last Stages of Life

Reflections on War

Inspired by Nature

Contentment in a Sunbeam

The sun on my shoulders
is warmer than a stole,
a comfort to the spirit
and warmth to my soul.

Reading my book,
I see the words with such clarity,
a quiet spot,
away from the crowd,
to be enjoyed gratefully.

A Bruised Reed I Will Not Break ...

A lesson learned
from a friend who arranged my wedding flowers:
if flower stems are bent or bruised,
when given a support
will continue to flourish.

When Edith's Amaryllis
fell over and bent
just prior to blooming,
together we worked
on attaching a supporting stick,
tying it with a ribbon.

A few days later
a beautiful white flower bloomed,
bringing joy at its complete recovery.

Edith Baillie with Amaryllis in full bloom

Spiritual Moments in Nature

Relaxing on my back deck under a tree,
depressed by yet another major dental expense,
a bird chirping a song,
moved at my presence,
branch by branch,
not further away,
instead, closer to me.

One bird after another
flew over and sat on a bare tree,
till a whole flock had joined
watching intently,
overlooking in silent respect
at a young priest's burial ceremony.

A fox came to
yet another burial ceremony,
as a Chaplain was speaking
she noticed no one paying attention,
then looking around
discovered the fox circling, stretching, then settling
on the grave next to them,
then continued on with the ceremony.

Crawford Lake Musings

*H*iking in
early December,
gray, threatening skies,
trees bare of their leaves,
nature in reflection
between two seasons.

The bounty of colors have left us,
drawing attention to life's bare bones,
brilliant green moss carpeting rocks,
cedar trees, roots as fingers grasp at boulders,
finding moisture in cracks and crevices,
clinging on to life,
flourishing against all odds.

Tree stumps,
ghosts of their strong pasts,
with ripples,
demonstrate nature's adapting
a wire fence
integrated into the tree's growth.
Another tree fallen,
with roots scattered wide, yet flat,
demonstrate that roots
need to grow deep
to hold on during life's turbulences.

As nature pauses and adapts
in myriad ways,
so can I.

Trees in Need of Love

Words are needed about our trees,
capturing their beauty, constancy, let's show them our love,
value their contributions, their changes and adapting,
they add variety of scenery, enhance our well-being,
providing shade on a hot day,
lowering temperatures in buildings and streets,
a place to climb, a provider of fruit, nuts, flowers and leaves,
wood for furniture, buildings and carvings,
a home for insects, birds and animals, a place for lovers to pose,
a wedding photo shoot scenic provider followed by family pictures,
a way to celebrate a birth or memorialize a loved one,
give strength to hilly landscapes and ravines,
holding up our soil and roads.
Trees need our love
expressed in real ways,
proper choice
and placement,
a spread of roots
not covered in cement,
faithful watering, and trimming.
The will to do and not just talk,
join in declaring our love requires
a commitment which no tax break will bring.

Imagine a World ...

*W*here we knew instinctively like Canadian geese,
who should best lead,
the rest following in perfect formation
to achieve harmony in flight.

Queens would be there,
just like the queen bees know
to increase their hive comes from helping
the community around to flourish and grow.

Like Penguins, fathers would know
that childcare is not just a concern for women,
but a responsibility for both parents.

Bears too teach to eat what sustains and nourishes you,
then learn to hibernate
when you need time-out during winter's worst storms.

Then like the armies of ants,
working in harmony,
moving together loads bit by bit.

Humankind is seen
as the most intelligent of creatures,
yet why do we have so much to learn
from all other species?

Chasing Clouds

*D*ays of drought,
humid, energy-draining hours,
I drive home,
fascinated by the cloud formations
evolving billows,
filling the dusk sky with shades of grey, purple, pink and green,
my windshield a constantly changing viewmaster of
the clouds' mirrored formations
as reflections on water,
evidence of rainfalls, puddles and spatters,
I see downpours in the distance
waiting,
yet straining forward to a blessing
of refreshing rain
renewal to the earth
and to a life's drought.

Goose, Penguins and Squirrel lessons

*F*ather goose
rarely gets mentioned,
yet stands by the side
of Mother goose while nesting,
leaving to get food and nourishment,
returning to stand along side during
February`s temperamental weather:
rain, sleet and snow,
in the long wait for goslings.

A CIBC bank commercial
treading carefully in showing
males and females
working in harmony
doing all the tasks a home demands,
of laundry, cleaning and childcare,
focussing on penguins,
more advanced in their practices
of equality amongst the sexes.

A squirrel caught on video
doing a dance in the snow,
showing delight in the
joy and beauty of a change of season.

Birds and animals
we watch and
take delight in,
learn from their examples
of how to make life worth living.

Rocks as Pets

*I*n jest Gary Dahl suggested, when friends in the bar complained
about high-maintenance pets, how much work they created,
perhaps you should adopt a Pet Rock instead!

What happened next, an idea's success unexplained
as he gave each Pet Rock originating in Rosarito Beach, Mexico,
a cardboard home with straw bed, air holes and instructions for care.

Originating in 1975,
the following months led to 1.5 million in Pet Rock sales,
two tons worth of rocks!
While this fast frenzied pace of sales did not last, the Pet Rock endured
in fond collective memory of an idea that spread like fire.
An amazing feat for sure,
at a time long before widespread internet use,
facebook, twitter, pinterest, ipads, cellphones with WIFI and cameras.
Unlike the expression that one can't see the forest for the trees,
he pointed out to us the meaning in small enduring things,
no two rocks are imitations of each other,
each has its own personality, color, size and feel,
now expressed with painting faces of people and insects,
animals and birds on rocks,
a touchstone with significant words to hold onto through rough times:
forgive, love, believe, relax, wisdom, cherish, love, honor.
the burden of a farmer or gardener's existence
interrupting a plow or shovel's work, thrown to the side,
at times arranged into fences, for barn or home foundations,
form exterior walls of homes, indoor or outdoor fireplaces,
now recognized as an integral garden decoration.
Reinforcements for river and creek beds, roadsides,
garden ponds and lakeshores.

Rockpiles, with rocks balanced one by one with precision and skills,
the appearance of Inukshuks, an Inuit tradition, a welcoming greeting,
have travelled down south, adding interest to roadsides,
gardens and lakeshores.

While it is hard to know for sure,
I can't help but consider that Gary's Pet Rocks enabled people
to look at rocks differently,
showing appreciation for their beauty and individuality.

Home and Community Life

How to Feel Young Again

At my grade school reunion
my grade one teacher
handed me a picture of myself
from that time.

Without a purse or pocket,
I put it down,
found by her,
I was rebuked,
bringing me back in time,
getting a scolding from my Grade one teacher.

A Parking Ticket Ordered

$\mathcal{T}$he night of my
second child's birth
I ordered my husband
to get a parking ticket
and he did.

Within an hour of the birth,
he had wanted to move his truck
to avoid getting a ticket.
Not wanting him to leave
at such an intense time,
I ordered him to stay.

One of my high school teachers
was present for his child's birth
vowing to never be there again,
as he couldn't handle witnessing
the pain, the blood, the drama of birth.

His feelings at this time matter little,
the necessity being present
to his wife during the birth process,
the joy of the new life of their offspring.

Bubbles Delight

first published in "Across the Generational Divide" Ont. Poetry Society Chapbook

A look of delight
I did see
sitting on the back stairs
of our apartment,
my two-year-old and me.

Taking turns
blowing bubbles
in the wind,
to drift and meander
as they please.

A woman
on the sidewalk
sauntering by,
had such a look of surprise
to find bubbles
floating around the corner,
drifting in the air.

Isolation and Connection

*H*ydro Outage in two thousand and three,
more serious than originally thought,
I and another middle manager
returned to the nursing home
to distribute lanterns to the washrooms and hallways,
fill tubs with water and give residents assurance.
We wondered why the maintenance manager
who lived so close by did not appear.
The reason unknown to us,
he was spending five hours
stuck alone in his apartment's elevator in the dark.

A policeman never felt such community support
as when this outage happened.
He directed a busy intersection's traffic,
a long eight hours in thirty-five celsius heat,
a variety of people handed him
ice cream, pop, and cold water
on a continuous basis
in expressions of gratitude.

Life's Chores

first published in Across the Generational Divide – Ontario Poetry Society Chapbook

*F*or my Tante Susan,
the greatest indignity
in nursing home living
was not being allowed
to make her visitors a cup of tea.

For another lady,
having staff members put away her laundry
signified her loss of autonomy.

Not able to make an occasional meal,
take care of doing your own dishes
or coax a family member to do their share.

The chores we fight over and begrudge,
all the daily routines,
when no longer available,
we miss as
there is comfort
in our ability to do life's chores.

Language no Barrier

*dedicated to my friend, Izaura Parda
and in memory of her former boss, Mr. Ronald Osborne*

A friend I made on the flight back from Brazil
with no similar language
yet a connection was made.

Then continued on
when her boss with a generous heart
to someone who
be-friended his housekeeper / nanny,
offered me a ride home
from the airport.

Thirty-two years later
our friendship lives on.

Community Connections

based on a CBC radio "In the Field" story by David Gutnick

A young Irish woman fled across the water,
abused and hunted by her father,
found and killed in the town of Geel in Belgium.
What good could possibly come
when her desperation and fear,
ended in tragedy?

This story from the seventh century
on these traumatic events,
resulted in her being named St. Dimpna,
Patron Saint of the mentally ill,
her life inspiration for the townspeople of Geel
to welcome people
developmentally challenged
and mentally ill to blend in.

A long tradition for centuries following
of families taking adults in their homes
in need of love, work, friendship and community.
When institutionalization
became a worldwide norm,
the town of Geel had a say
in showing another way.

Giving this inspiring story further thought,
my Uncle Gerrit with developmental challenges
in neighboring Holland
benefited from this practice.
Forty years he spent working on a farm,
accepted as a part of a family,
pride in his contributions to this world, in this place.

Making Applesauce Sweeter

in memory of Dirk and Rie Jongkind

The way to make applesauce sweet
without adding sugar,
put in a variety of different apples.

This advice from an older friend,
perhaps
applies to their life as well as applesauce.

When her ninety-four year old husband
celebrated his birthday,
he was surrounded by people of a variety of cultures.

Their lives made sweeter
and enriched by having
friends of a variety of ages and backgrounds.

Divorce in the Sixties

*W*hen couples divorced
in the nineteen sixties,
with the stigmatization of divorce,
the children felt the ripples of waves of blame
for their parents' actions.
The school didn't know what to do with them,
the community awash in gossip,
was not a supporting place to
gain strength through a difficult time.

Surrounding families and friends affected,
allegiances drawn
ostracization enacted.

Marital struggles parents go through,
attempted to hide,
The children
are more aware than we think,
having to struggle through
all the emotions in dealing
with their parents issues.

November Days Appreciated

I used to dread November,
the gloomiest of months,
after the beauty of fall colours,
awaiting the freshness of a clean snowfall.

I was given a different mindset
when I asked the senior residents
of the nursing home where I worked
their thoughts on:
Why I like November?

The crisp coolness of November days
without having to deal with the worry of snow and ice.
The comfort of dressing in warm sweaters and layers.
Remnants of the fall colours last well into the month.
The purple, grey skies of the sunsets
with the bare-naked trees all have a special beauty all their own.

When the sun does come out after grey days
we appreciate it so much more.
A time to appreciate soups, stews, home baking,
attend Bazaars and the Royal Winter Fair.

Inside our homes seem cozier as the night
comes earlier and weather gets cooler.
We need to deal with the sadness of Remembrance Day first,
before we can get to the joy and happiness of Christmas.

I vow to appreciate all the variances
of scenery, new comforts and weather in November.

Dealing with Losses

Don't let yourself get too close
advice I was told,
but ignored
as in my first job in an infirmary
a third of my active residents
died in my time there.

At my next job, less deaths at first
but each year averaged out to one-quarter, a fraction
of the population died or moved out.
Blessings received in life lessons
I learned from each.

Each person recognized
with a picture posted and a card to sign
and a paragraph
in newsletter and fond memories book,
if not well known to myself
I found others who
acknowledged their individuality.

Victims of guns,
numbered every year,
each leaving a hole in their community,
losses of a son, brother,
spouse, daughter, sister, mother,
father, grandson/granddaughter,
friend, schoolmate, worker.

A member of an international aid team
helping in wartime relief,
overcome with emotion
at handling bodies of young children
decided to talk to them,
address them as if still living,
as they worked at this arduous task.

The Huronia Centre
had it all wrong,
ignoring individuals deaths,
relegating them to a number,
explaining their absence:
they've gone farm way,

Loss of life,
when treated indifferently,
dehumanizes individuals,
ignoring the loss of their contribution
to family and community,
ultimately
diminishes all
in our
potential in being fully human.

The Photos We Didn't Take

first published in "Across the Generational Divide" Ontario Poety Society Chapbook

After doing
renovations or demolition
in our eagerness to see the new,
we realize later our neglect
to have photos
of how it used to be.

My brother-in-law
was going to do a painting
of our family's old barn
but was left totally confused
with too many conflicting views
of how it used to be.

Areas of dispute, sources of family arguments:
whether we once had hogs enjoying
life in the mud outside
in a lean-to attached to the barn.
Also the direction of the corncribs
I know for sure was east-west
while my father disagrees
insisting they were north-south.

Gradually we are becoming
like my grandparents in past years
having arguments on who is right
about how things used to be.

While no professional artist
I did a drawing of the old barn.
If anyone disputes my facts
can take a pencil
to record and keep what
they think are their accurate
memories intact.

A Necessary Detail Omitted

My sister's classmate
was a fun-loving joker,
well-liked class clown.
He tried to follow the norm.
pretending he was the same
but ...
in middle age he committed suicide
a year before the class reunion.

A tribute to him
was placed in the anniversary booklet,
the reason why he was so tortured
to commit suicide was left out.

He was a gay man
in a world unfriendly
to people who differ from the norm.

As in the past ...
redheads were ostracized,
people from other religions or cultures vilified.
A mixed marriage in the fifties
was between a Catholic and a Protestant,
a reason to be kicked out of the family.
The yellow fever talked about in 1914 newspapers
fearing the influx of Chinese,
a lack of gratitude and acknowledgement for
putting our country together by their work on the railroad.
As people with disabilities were needed to be hidden from view,
not offered a job in workplaces – and still are not.

Change, coming in bits and pieces, needs to keep rolling in.

Celebrate the Real

Let's celebrate the real, rather than perfection,
a couple deciding to join together in matrimony,
handling negotiations between two families' interests,
able to make compromises,
to come to agreement and assert their own values,
budget and priorities between the two partners.

A home decorated
to be worthy of a magazine spread show
should rather be a reflection of the interests, creativity
and day-to-day needs, availability of money
of its inhabitants.

Family now redefined
takes various forms,
no longer solely those sharing blood:
roommates, friends, acquaintances and children
who have grown to be one's closest ties,
people who support our growth as human beings.

A vehicle of choice:
a bicycle, car, electric or gas, motorcycle, public transit,
the method we choose
should be about our individual and family needs,
our budget and time constraints,
concern for reducing our environmental impact.

In politics and workplaces,
the way to work things out
initially will not appear to be most efficient
when taking the time to include the voices,
the wisdom of more citizens and employees.

Small Pleasures

*W*hen the big issues in life come our way
understanding why, how,
where and who
escapes us,
reasons for life happenings
that never come.

Think small
in finding pleasure,
the friendship and support of others,
the warm comforts of home,
a cup of tea, a glass of wine
homemade soup, a nourishing meal,
fresh baked goods from the oven,
a hot soothing shower, a warm bed,
the familiarity of favorite underwear and socks,

The beauty of nature in winter,
trees that glisten in the sun,
a fresh blanket of snow
signifying a new start,
a breath of fresh air
crisp, cool and clean
a walk to clear out anxious thoughts.
A chance to ski
zoom down a hill
with grace and ease
surrounded by a chorus of trees.

Joy found in small pleasures
is what gives us the will to carry on
when answers to life's questions elude us
a response in the discovery is – *Let it be, let it be.*

Lessons Learned

*W*hat I learned from horseback riding
was that when bucked off, get right back on
so your last memory will
be a good one.

From riding a bicycle on
my cycling trips,
when approaching a big hill,
don't look up,
take on just what is right in front of you.
Having the company of others
can encourage you to do far
more than you expected.

On my canoe trips,
I learned to be close
with nature
is to be in touch with myself.

What I know from walking
is that it beats driving
to notice all
the little pleasures of nature,
remain in touch with my community.

From traveling to other countries
one sees there are other ways of doing things.
People with less possessions
are often more generous and welcoming.
Others know how to consume less of the world's resources,
being happier than us.

Coming Back in with my Own Laundry

A Russian proverb wisely states:
If we were to hang our problems
along with those of others
on the clothesline,
we still would come back in
with our own laundry.

Recalling bad things
that have happened to me,
comparing with friends, family
or those unemployed or with health concerns
for longer periods of time
or have lost children, brothers, sisters,
a wife or husband,
involved in car accidents, fires, explosions, floods.

I still prefer
to be me
and the laundry I own:
my problems,
I can deal with them
with support and guidance
from friends and family
along life's way.

Our Quest for Perfection

A new life is seen as perfect,
no scars or irregularities must be evident.

A new environment with new buildings
and improved design
will not erase all social problems.

A new marriage must
be celebrated with a perfect wedding day,
even though all that follows will not be perfect.

Renovations shows
details us on how to create the perfect home
seeming to forget people have to live in it,
have places to put
reading material, books, magazines,
with some family pictures.

All who like to appear to be having
a perfect family life,
will have that allusion shattered from time to time.
As having the perfect job
will have its many moments of difficulties
and unforeseen changes.
A perfectly planned retirement
can quickly change with unexpected events or diagnosis.

Let go of the perfection illusion
and live life,
making the choices that reflect our values
in tune with the reality of our existence.

Money where Their Heart is

*M*y great-aunt
often knit for children abroad,
when she turned one hundred
gave her remaining money
to Albert Schweitzer Hospital in Africa.

A retired man
had served on numerous boards,
held many positions of leadership,
paid attention to others needs
along life's way,
had a fondness for Brazil
where his family spent a few years.
On his passing,
his family asked for all donations
in his memory to go to Amazon Medical center.

A well-loved volunteer
known around the Nursing Home
made quite a creative splash at the Home's Fashion Shows,
her cheerful smile and steady presence
contributing to get residents
to foot care and chapel services alike.
At life's closing asked for donations
for the Heart and Stroke foundation.

While everyone can be replaced,
no one comes around and contributes
in quite the same way.
Names may be forgotten,
legacies of memories and impact
on lives they touched will live on.

A Reward on Earth

A reward on Earth
was given in the last year of
a single woman's life.
She acted like a mother hen
to her resident neighbors
in the area on her floor
and also to the staff.

In the years before
an active children's aid society in her province,
she took over her mother's business
of being a foster mother over many years
to over two hundred children,
some for a few weeks or months
when a mother was ill, unable to cope,
others for as long as a year,
paid often in barter
with food or services rendered.

A thirteen year old volunteer
came into her life,
appreciated and cared for her,
acting like a daughter
or granddaughter of her own
she never had.

Two weeks before she died
she was showered with Christmas gifts,
experiencing
the love and appreciation
she so deserved.

A Prank or a Vision?

from a CBC radio story

A seemingly thoughtless act
by a teenager
who decided to collapse,
pretending to have a heart attack
at the local Blockbuster's Video Store,
having the ambulance called to a neighborhood
where they were most needed ...

As a young father,
returning from a hike with his wife and two boys,
collapsed on his driveway from a heart attack,
was resuscitated shortly after
by the paramedics
in that same ambulance
that happened to be close by
due to this prank.

The father recovered
with a grateful wife and family,
the following year added another child
who came to be, because of
perhaps, not a prank
but a vision
by a teenager who was never located,
to be thanked personally
for saving a life.

The We Don't Want to Know Department

*T*he Canadian Government in the nineteen twenties
fired the Chief Medical Officer for suggesting
native children were dying
in large numbers in residential schooling,
then started a policy of no longer recording
how and why children were disappearing.

One would like to think society is constantly progressing,
increasing awareness and knowledge,
yet still run up against walls built up
by authorities who *just don't want to know*
supported by people hiding behind walls of indifference,
if it doesn't affect them personally, *why should they care?*

A ditty Louis Kamookak, a Nunavit-Inuk historian
was taught in Residential Schools:

What did you learn in school today,
dear little boy of mine?
I learned that our government
must be strong.
They're always right
*and never wrong.**
shows how disconnected the government was
from first nations children's reality,
not able to return to their parents daily,
obliteration of value in their culture, language and points of view,
those who were teaching were unwilling to learn.

ironically part of a protest song by Tom Paxton

Toothless thru the Ages

*first published in "Across the Generational Divide", Ont.Poets Society Chapbook,
also in Canadian Stories Magazine, Vol.18*

A grade one student loses their first tooth
proudly displayed, donated to the tooth fairy,
awaits a reward.

In my twenties, three teeth lost
in a roller skating accident
upset at the loss of parts, changed facial features
and ever-expanding costs.

Three nursing home residents
at the same time lost one front tooth,
I asked for a group picture
but respected their choice to refuse.

In my fifties, one spring after years of use
I replaced one bridge,
that autumn had my front tooth cap fall off,
needing another bridge all in one year.

Continued on working, giving tours of the seniors home
minus my front tooth,
explaining *I'm in the midst of dental care.*

My son, a teenager
partially chipped off his front tooth
refused to meet with friends until repaired,
*that's fine to go out toothless when old
not when you are young like me.*

Still he posted his toothless grin
on Facebook for all in his world to see.

Numbered Graves

*I*n Texas,
numbers are put on
the convicts graves,
as the state ending their lives,
depriving people of names,
is the way to strip people of
their humanity and places of origin
and how they got there.

A similar tactic
used in Ontario's Huronia Institution,
if we don't acknowledge
their names with their birth and death date,
we don't have to admit
that humans are buried here,
how inhuman we were
in our treatment of
those deemed not worthy of care.

When five thousand children died in China's Earthquake
due to shoddy construction of their schools,
the artist Ai Wei Wei
insisted on putting names
to the numbers with birth dates,
he wanted to create a visual show
of the harm done by negligence.

Three Intersecting Stories

On Day One: the sentencing of a drunk driver,
three children and a grandfather's lives ended.
Parents struggle with
unimaginable loss, trying to carry on.
The driver's choice changes forever
families and communities,
theirs and his own.

Day Two: the funeral and celebration of life of a popular politician,
often inebriated,
respecting the taxpayer,
rarely wanted to be chauffeured.

Both from families of priviledge
blinds us to the realities:
addictions and heavy drinking
have an origin,
a large percentage with past abuse.

Not confined to one class,
financial or educational status,
abuse happens
from people least expected:
any in our social circles
of family, friends, neighbours,
teachers, coaches, religious figures.

Day Three: an abusive hockey usher charged,
hundreds of victims.
Our society didn't take seriously,
or learn life lessons.
Three stories, intersecting streams.

The Nails of my Home

When making renovations to house and home,
nails of assorted sizes found:
a railway pin under our driveway,
long nails, square nails, roofing nails, rusty nails, short nails.

Each nail had its place in keeping our home together:
a railway pin – enabled an ability to travel,
to make connections to other people and places,
long nails joining multiple boards and surfaces together,
roofing nails in keeping shingles on to protect our home from the elements,
square nails originally used when the house was made,
short nails for small joinings.

What are the nails that have kept our home together,
through tears, struggles, pain, losses of finances,
dignity, health and well-being:
connecting past and present,
year after year, day by day through many a battering storm?
Nails of patience, faith, love, understanding,
perseverance, caring, and knowledge, that we can make it through
despite all the forces that threaten to tear us apart.

Bad News Overload

Sometimes we want to shut off the news,
we just don't want to hear it any more,
we don't want to know
of ours or our neighbouring countries brewing troubles,
as it can worry us so,
adding to our personal anxieties,
we know what happens out there can come creeping closer.

Yet to not stay in touch,
remain uninvolved in the world surrounding,
is not an option when we are constantly interacting,
utilizing others goods and services.
Being willfully uninformed just can't work,
pressing issues need well-timed reactions.

Having timeout from the news
occasionally provides respite,
considering the alternative:
countries where press freedoms are severely restricted,
the only information given is the government's official story.

Closing our ears and eyes,
to remain uninvolved in the surrounding world
shutting our feeling and reasoning
can we really say: *we just didn't know it was happening?*

The Human Family Responds

At times
in the midst of troubles
we do not always share
all the details with family members or friends.
Or if we do, they are unable
to be available when most needed.

Friends or family may
have awareness
but may be unable to respond
due to work commitments,
time restraints or
family or health issues
of their own.

Yet others
can move in closer
acquaintances suddenly
fill our needs
in unexpected ways.

We never know who
in the human family
will respond to us.

Women's Craft group in 1988 at Blair Court

Life at Work

Compliments and Insults

When getting compliments I don't deserve,
I pass on to another,
but also gratefully receive,
because in this life
many insults or criticism also get sent my way,
for things beyond my control
done by others actions or words.

When tempted to take
my anger out on a frontline staff,
it is good to remember
to be as tactful as can be,
as they also
may not deserve the criticism
which others should get.

A compliment given,
an outlet of appreciation,
joy to the receiver and giver alike.

Agents of Change or Stagnation

A gents of change
will be rejected, ignored,
misunderstood by the masses.

A time of reward
for sticking to one's principles,
not always seen in political or work life.

The alternative: letting things be,
takes its toll
as the daily assaults on
one's ego and integrity,
internalized anger,
health problems arrive
threatening to keep one from life.

Often the agents of change
are first, third or tenth,
to push for improvements.

One gets it started, others continue on,
yet others bring to completion
the job that needs to get done.

This too will pass ... this too will pass ...

A poster in my former nursing home office
was good to focus on,
when we had so many restrictions
put on during weeks of quarantines.

A phrase to focus on
when we go through rough times,
but also
for the moments in time
when you feel you have arrived
at a place of contentment,
achievement and completeness.

I make gratitude my attitude
cherish what I have
as I know that this too will pass,
as cracks of chaos can appear.
In life like dominos
things can easily be knocked down.

One realizes then
how much social supports you lean on:
spouse, children, parents, siblings, co-workers and friends,
that all do their part
in making it manageable
to continue on in our lives.

The Emperor's New Clothes

Deference to authorities
should it be a thing of the past?
When people were afraid to correct,
question or express another viewpoint
to Royalty, Politicians, their bosses, Doctors and Police.

Authorities or celebrities
when surrounded with yes-men and women,
get a false view of their place in the world
and how things really are,
when not rubbing and polishing their brains
with those of alternate views.

The Job That Gave Her a Landing

first published in Canadian Stories Magazine, 2015

A new immigrant in the 1950's,
checking out the employment centre for jobs,
came home and told her father
the one job she could apply for was an elevator operator,
thought she should wait for something better.

Her father sent her back to apply for this job,
initially taken by another,
was asked to leave her name and number.

The person originally hired lasted a day and left,
so this woman was hired in her place.

She used this new job
to make small talk
with each person entering the elevator,
improving her english skills.

Lasting a year in this job,
she later looked fondly back
at the relationships formed
in this, the best job she ever had.

The Picker Upper

A resident moved in to the nursing home
with the help of an acquaintance.
In the eight years she lived there,
she had few visitors.

Decorating the fireplace mantel for Easter
one by one the bunnies
disappeared into her room
and I would take them back.

A china cabinet she had with lock and key,
filled with figurines
collected over her years.

Was her picker-upper habit
one that developed along with her dementia,
or was it a lifelong habit
that made her lose friends and acquaintances as
they noticed things missing after her visit?

After she died
her niece donated the cabinet
and contents to the home, items auctioned off to staff,
with the three wooden monkeys remaining behind:
hear no evil, see no evil, speak no evil,
placed on top of the TV
– to be recognized by a cleaning staff
who knew exactly whose it had been;
a resident long gone, who she had
helped search everywhere for it
years before.

The Proper Way

The proper way
I've always been told
is to go through the right channels,
up the management chart
with issues needing addressing,
then satisfaction will be achieved.

Instead there can be a stubborn
unwillingness
for those who have been appointed to lead,
to consider paying attention
to those they don't consider worthy
of consideration.

When one comes across
complete silence,
an unwillingness to communicate,
more is going on,
a perpetuation of the class system
when no demands
are put on those in decision making roles
to have two-way communications
with others than those they've appointed the head.

———

When getting no response,
it is best to make alliances:
finding strength in numbers,
in putting forward serious concerns,
for all who have a vested interest.

The Reasons Why

*W*hen we see emotional, irrational behaviour,
whether in children or adults,
the reason unknown to us.

A child told he will never be returning home,
will be placed in foster care,
broke every window in the childrens aid office,
medication was seen as mandatory
rather than empathy for his strong emotions
that came with the enormity of this life change.

It is rarely what's seen on the surface,
as a calm-looking river masks a strong current underneath.
It is the person reacting to their own or family history,
recent or traumatic events in their lives,
the emotions that come bubbling up,
surfacing in unexpected ways.

The Bakery Men's First Job

Of my Dad and his three brothers,
   all but one were horse lovers.
      The reason for this?

      Dad's early memories of
   his youngest brother at seven,
   riding his horse round in circles,
   keeping it walking for long hours
      operating the *Rosmolen*
   powering the bread dough mixer,
   trying to stop from falling asleep.

      This task he took over from
         his older brother,
perhaps instigating their belief in bakery automation.

Reasons to Work

Not everyone in circumstances
to work jobs they love
nor could we be provided
with all the goods and services
that provide life's necessities
if this was every worker's philosophy.
Other reasons to carry on:
providing a living for self and family,
allowing pursuits of outside interests:
developing their creativity,
time for volunteer work, ability to travel,
funding their own or children's,
spouse or siblings education,
have a lifestyle that gives enough
attention to their significant relationships
of family and friends.

Many in repetitive jobs in food, services or products delivery
have esteem in knowing they
are providing necessary services to society,
enjoy the contact with others, working in a team
or the clients they interact with,
may appreciate the closeness of their workplace to their home,
take pride in doing a quality job with attention to detail,
appreciate the feedback they get.
Even people working in jobs they love,
can find the peripheral costs of staying
take over any enjoyment they once had,
long working hours, unrecognized efforts,
frustrating systems, less autonomy,
coercive bosses,
less pride in making a difference.

Literature and Movies

Books for a Reason

A thoughtful book by Robert Coles,
last of the
Children of the Crisis series:
"The Privileged Ones –
The well-off in America"
inspired my interest in
traveling to Brazil.

Other books too
have come into my life,
offering insights,
preparing me for experiences
I soon would go through.

Emotional intelligence,
a gift reading brings
to prepare you to deal with everything.

Pockets for Grudges

inspired by a book – The Grudge Keeper by Mara Rockliff, illustrated by Eliza Wheeler

A customer of the Toy Store
described a doll for her grandson she had bought,
with a number of pockets,
hiding places for small items:
a zippered mouth, behind the ear,
pockets in shirt, pants, socks and shoes
and was looking for tiny treasures to store in each place.

That same day, treating myself
to buying a children's book with life lessons:
The Grudge Keeper which tells of a man
who made a habit of keeping
all his own and others grudges,
which accumulated to such volume
they filled every corner of his house,
until a whirlwind arrived which blew all the grudges out.

A lesson for all who are keepers of grudges,
filling all nooks and crannies
up to capacity.
Knowing we are both recipients and holders of grudges,
as we can never fully understand
the reasons for what others think and do,
as we haven't had their experiences.
We can hear their perspectives and try,
but also deal with each issue of conflict
with more generosity.

Dying Broke

I aim to die broke,
Bob Barker said
as he wants all money he made
in this life to be spread
to causes of his choosing,
so his ideas and values will continue on.

In the movie, *Black Book*,
a seeming friend of the Jews,
instead a traitor, when discovered,
attempts to leave the country,
hidden in a coffin,
surrounded with money and jewels,
dies as he aimed,
with ill-gotten gains covering him
from head to toe,
the uselessness of his greed,
put on display.

A common fear
for many throughout their life,
is to have others or their government
to obtain all their riches,
making every effort to retain all they can
when perhaps to die broke
is the best aim for all man and womankind.
We enter this world
without a penny to our name,
why take more than you need
when you can leave this world a better place,
money spent in the right directions
till the end of your days.

Flight of the Innocent

Kidnappings
previously associated
with countries such as
Columbia, Italy, Mexico,
have also occurred in my city and
in my hometown,
now a worldwide phenomenon.

Flight of the Innocent – an Italian movie
about a young boy in a kidnapper's family
which spoke some truths.

The point
so poignantly shown in the movie,
the family members of wrongdoers
should not always share the blame,
especially children
should not be tarnished,
shunned, banned
and withdrawn from
society's assistance.
Rather encouraged
to be all they can be,
without living in dark shadows
of their parents or siblings.

A Claimed Treasure

inspired by one of Facebook 10th Anniversary stories and my travels in Brazil

An Unclaimed Treasure,
a euphemism of past use,
to describe a woman staying unattached
into her later adult years,
is the moniker I would like to revise,
to describe Raimundo Arrudo Sobrinho.

For thirty-five years homeless,
nineteen years on an island he resided,
in Sao Paulo, Brazil,
barely noticed as street traffic whizzed by.
Until a young woman, Shalla Montiero
befriended him, impressed with his poetry
and his dream to publish a book one day,
set up a Facebook page called *The Conditioned*,
to give his publishing a start.
His admirers increased,
no longer shy to stop by and chat,
or put off by his lack of hygiene,
a fault he admitted to in a poem,
"physical hygiene and mental hygiene, here,
I don't know which is harder to practice".
But the renewed contact most valued
that resulted was someone younger,
who longed to know what
had happened to his big brother.
Re-united at last,
once again a part of his family,
the beam on his face
outshone his haircut, shave and new clothes,
at being recognized and valued for all that he is,
loved and appreciated as a Claimed Treasure.

Accusations of Snuggling

A typo was made, then corrected,
in the book *The Devil's Highway*,
describing Mexicans following the path north,
in which Luis Alberto Urrea stated,
a vast conspiracy of snuggling,
the spelling was changed but should it?

A definition – *when people are snuggling,*
there are no personal boundaries between the two;
to draw or press closely against for a lengthy period of time.

When it comes to this migration,
Mexican government and US corporate bosses
share the responsibility, with border enforcements,
a planned cement wall unworkable.

Taxes paid by illegals: sales and food,
water, hydro, federal and state taxes.

Three billion per year added to the US economy,
a study by UCLA's North American Integration
and Development Centre.

The movie *A Day without Mexicans* demonstrates
how dependent the US is on Mexico
for keeping food costs down,
contributing labour and skills
on farms, homes and industries.

The states of California, Texas, Arizona,
and New Mexico once belonged to Mexico,
now Trump saying Mexicans
presence no longer wanted.

South of the Mexican border,
close to one million American retirees live permanently.

An inter-dependent relationship exists,
benefiting both,
their roots intertwined, providing growth.

Into the Spotlight

*inspired by the actions of journalists of "The Spotlight" at the Boston Globe, made into a movie *quote from this movie*

It takes a village to raise a child,
an oft repeated remark,
yet at times,
*it also takes a village to ignore abuse of children,**
of so many who
look the other way.
Those who do not want to upset
the powers that be
in places in sports, religion, education, business
or high standing in their community.

A common tactic to dismiss or not investigate suspicions,
the concerns of a powerless child,
who lacks concentration abilities,
or an adult with addictions, lack of maturity,
a self-image or weight problem, poor self-care,
calling it an isolated incident,
perhaps done only once or twice,
acting as if it is of no consequence.

At first sex abuse
was seen as mainly female experiences,
how easy it was to dismiss their claims,
now society is gradually recognizing,
it is also devastating for males.

Fly Seizure Boy Fly

based on a Toronto Star story by Donna Tranquada, Rick's friend

I've learned that people will forget what you said,
people will forget what you did,
but people will never forget how you made them feel,
Maya Angelou remarked.

Seizure Boy, a cartoon character Rick Barnsley created,
a superhero who flies to others rescue.
Unreal, yet so true
in all the lives he touched and blessed
with friendly welcomes and companionship,
infectious in his love of art,
contributer to life in community.

Perhaps a quality noticed
by the Prime Minister Harper's entourage,
who wanted to have a political photo op,
posing with Rick,
the PM too busy to have time to get to know his name,
or that it was a bag of weed he was carrying,
or check the ArtHeart program
which helped him and others to flourish creatively.
A life interrupted at age eight with tragedy,
a car accident both parents killed, causing a learning disability,
needing to learn to read, write and walk again,
with seizures a life-long reminder.
With the love of a grandmother and older brother who
assisted him through his earliest struggles,
till he was able to live independently.

Maya, who predeceased him by a few weeks,
most surely described Rick accurately,
a man who left those whose lives he touched
in warm feelings all around for those in his community.

The Chaplain and the Executioner

*I*n the documentary, *Into the Abyss*
the death penalty is displayed,
a simple cure to solve society's ills,
in Texas vengeance is theirs,
clinging on to old testament beliefs.

A Chaplain who was there
for many convicts' last moments,
tears in his eyes
recounting the many faces of
those guilty and innocent,
standing in front
of the rows on rows of numbered graves
in the prison cemetery.

The Executioner described in detail
how he carried out his job,
strapping the convicted in,
recording how long it took each to die,
the removal of the body.

As his recounting went on
his emotions spilled out
about the time he took the life of a female convict,
then having a breakdown,
a vision followed of all the convicts
in whose death he had played a part.
A turning point made,
leaving job security and pension behind,
financially set back,
his soul regained.

Paulo Coeho's Best Story

*I*n this movie
retracing the emotional
landscape of his life,
a car accident seriously injuring another,
set off his authoritarian Father,
to react harshly to many late teen and twenties actions,
authorizing shock treatments,
time in a mental hospital.

As a writer,
he was encouraged
to turn his thoughts
into words for songs,
another claimed credit,
setting off a mental breakdown.

Yet
it was the words of his song,
put him in touch
with his true reason for writing:
to connect people's emotions, enable understanding
which brought
healing to the relationship
of Father and Son.

His Father apologizing
finally understanding,
appreciating the talents
of his playwright, song-writer and author
of best selling books son.

The Music Played On ...

inspired by the movie: "Spring 1941" and the book "The Cellist of Sarejevo"

*I*n times of war the need to make compromises
to integrity, honesty and self-worth,
constant adjustments to save life and limb
of self, family or friends.

A commonly told story of women's bodies used
to gain special favours for life to hold onto,
was taken to other dimensions
in the movie: *Spring 1941,*
a Doctor and a Cellist and their daughter
are hidden by the vegetable seller.

Men too
were put into impossible situations,
compromises made, necessary routes taken.
Those who did the moral thing to try to save lives,
often got blamed for the collateral damage they survived.

Clara Planck, the cellist of Poland, returned thirty years later
to much fanfare and applause
despite seemingly insurmountable sorrows,
reunited with places of painful memories
she found the courage to play on.

Many years later,
in Sarejevo, another war, another cellist
who witnesses the bombing deaths
of twenty-two neighbours in a bread line.
He too decided the music should go on,
and played for twenty-two days in a row,
to restore peace and comfort at a scene
of valued lives lost.

Ariana Deda playing Cello

Last Stages of Life

Grass Head Sock Puppet

*M*y daughter's school craft project
found new uses
in bringing a touch
of nature to a side table
during
a woman's final months and weeks.

The outside brought
inside
for full enjoyment,
as she savored the feeling:
running her fingers
over the grass hair,
keeping it trimmed, watered
and looking clever as can be.

An extra reason
to stay a little longer on earth,
to nurture the nature
she still felt connected to.

Mutually Beneficial Exchanges

$\mathcal{T}$he English as a Second Language graduating class,
tired of their in-class practices,
wanted to engage in real conversation,
came once a month
to the Seniors Home,
conversations flowed freely,
as these new immigrants
showed such respect
and valued the talks
they had with the senior residents.

Residents who spoke little
became engaged in long conversations,
showing interest in
these students worlds
where they came from.

The students when returning
back to class,
became nostalgic
for their extended families back home.

An emptiness partially filled
with these new valued relationships.

People will Do What we Never Dreamed they would Do

$\mathcal{A}$n entertainer
at the Senior's Home
prior to playing and singing the classic,
I'm forever blowing bubbles
provided vials of soap we handed out
for the seniors to blow bubbles.

Used in an unintended way,
as one drank it immediately
a lady so un-deserving
of having her mouth washed with soap,
a generous giver and doer for others,
thankfully no lasting ill effects.

The point of relaying
this experience
is to make it known
that from birth to one hundred and two,
humans will do
what we never dreamed they would do.

Things out of our expectations will happen
split seconds in time
that impact and alter futures,
well-being of self and others.
It is not just in children and teenagers,
but people their whole life through
will do what we never thought they would do.

Grandma's Life in Objects

inspired by a poster by Katelynn Allemang

A poster at the funeral home
displayed their Grandma's love
for others by
the collection of objects
from her home
that created loving memories.

Three flavours of popsicles,
she always had for grandchildren,
the nailpolish collection
she loved to decorate nails,
a full dishrack of plates, cups,
pots and pans used in creating delicious meals,
the caps and boots of Grandpa,
signified his presence,
orchids she nurtured to life and growth,
along with vegetables
grown in her garden.

Her life and love of others summed up
in these objects,
what a treasure trove was stored up
for her children and grandchildren
the memories of her home.

End of Life Regrets

*B*eing widowed young,
my Grandfather was warned
by his Mother
against marrying again
while his boys were young,
heeded her advice.

In his later years,
he thought,
he should not have listened,
waiting for his boys to grow up
to marry again.

Their housekeeper
was kind, loving, caring.
Yet he never
consulted with her
as he would have with a wife
about nuances, many decisions
of parenting his boys.

The Five Stages of Living

Anger, bargaining, denial,
depression and acceptance –
the five stages of dying,
as determined by Elizabeth Kubler-Ross,
could be described
as five stages while living.

Life as in death
does not follow any one script,
or take a predictable course
emotions arise
from a variety of events
we move forward,
we regress
like tides at the beach,
growth comes with pain,
a route we would not choose,
loss of dignity is a part of life:
birth, death
and many points in between.

This was brought from Holland from where my Father immigrated.
It was used to announce a death in the community at the
various street corners of his hometown.

How to acknowledge death?

*W*hen you reach the end of life's journey
having seen your final sunrise and sunset,
some look for another life anew,
reunited with ones they love,
reincarnation is what some believe,
others think death is the end of all existence.
How do you prefer to think of this end
to your time on earth?

Will they send out change of address cards
to announce you are gone to meet your maker?
Or will you have a dirt nap, go in the fertilizer business,
as you decide to push up daisies.
Will you cross the river, drift to the other shore
or decide to sleep with the fishes?
Will you bite the dust or buy the farm,
having gone farm way?
Or cash in your chips, give up the ghost,
or get a one-way ticket to be with the ancestors
going to the big mansion in the sky?
Are you going to dance the last dance,
kicking the bucket as you go?
Or get a one-way ticket
get your sprouted wings, joining the choir invisible
life in the clouds, creating rainbows in the sky?
Or check out to buy a pine condo,
pass on, cease to be, rest in peace,
expire into that good night.

Death, unmentionable in many circles,
euphemisms we choose
express our hopes, faith and fears.

More Life to Live

to my friend, Phil Thomas – written two weeks before he died

I still have sunrises to greet,
friends to enjoy,
meals to savor,
a lover to kiss,
hugs to be wrapped in,
music to keep time with,
photos of memories to reminisce,
comedy shows to laugh at,
experiences to relive,
travels to remember,
scenery to take in,
water to splash,
books to read,
artwork to create,
thank you cards to make
and send,
nature calls to answer,
phone calls to make,
robins to view at my window,
first signs of spring,
gratitude songs to sing,
sunsets to see.

Children at Funerals

*M*y two-month-old son
at my Grandfather's funeral,
was a comfort to my uncle.
An assurance that the circle of life
is continuing on.

My six-year-old son
seeing his friend in a casket,
talked to him and said
"René – are you in there?"

A resident of the senior's home,
well-loved by her extended family
of grandchildren and great-grandchildren,
had no children at her funeral.

Children can be invited,
have their wishes respected,
to be or not to
attend this farewell to a loved one.

Secrets of Longevity

A coincidence perhaps
or something more ...

The two most prolific writers of letters
in the nursing home
were both over a hundred.

Neither had families
in this country
or children of their own,
but had faithful loving friends.

They knew the importance
of keeping in touch
and remained disciplined
in corresponding,
showing care and concern for others,
sharing details of their own lives.

A tradition to follow
which holds the secret to longevity.

Not Ready Yet

When entering a nursing home
for placement
it is easy to think,
I'm not ready,
I'm not quite there yet.

The average age coming in
is now eighty-six,
most have serious health concerns
or body care needs
or decline in mental abilities
to deal with day-to-day issues.

We are not ever ready
for the next stage of life …
entering school, a first job,
buying a first car,
travel abroad, getting married,
having our first child,
we move forward,
give each new stage our best efforts.

What is different:
in most other life stages,
is about growing independence
an ability to strike out on our own,
but now in life's later years
we learn how truly inter-dependant we are,
perhaps in reflecting on all of our life's times,
true independence never was there.

Memories to Erase or Keep

For some it is the views
of their father, mother or partner's last years,
when Cancer or Parkinsons
took so much of their body strength
away.

For others it is Alzheimers
or increasing Dementia
which changed their personality so,
at times a mean, stubborn streak or cheapness,
grasping to hold on to last vestiges of independence,
comes out with a vengeance.

My cousin said it took a year or two
after his Father's death
to let these awful memories go
his last months, his body wasting away
remembering him as the strong and compassionate
Father that he used to be.

A plaque with a saying another cousin gave
her Father years ago
foretold his future with Alzheimers:
*"Dad you always went the extra mile
because you never stopped to ask for directions."*
showed his personality
of discovering life's potentials in the meanderings.

Memories Go, Feelings Remain

A senior with
Alzheimers' or Dementia
will not always
recognize a loved one,
be able to say their name or recall past times,
or yesterday's visit,
may think a sister or daughter
is their mother.

When asked:
Mom, do you know who I am?
One replied:
I don't know who you are,
but my heart knows.

Another once said:
I forget what I want to forget,
her way to block out painful memories,
unfortunately good memories went with them.

My children will not remember every good thing
I have done for or with them,
although having photographs helps,
but these things have added to
their general sense of well-being.

Just as a visit to a senior,
with no capacity to store new memories,
will sense someone visiting them cares,
adding to their feelings of
being connected to others.

For Those Left Behind

*M*any will wonder
could something have been done differently?
shock that it happened fast,
things that could have been said earlier,
conflicts that could have been resolved,
haunted by past angry words,
rage at their loved one for leaving,
trauma at unpleasant scenes imprinted in their memory,
guilt at their impatience during the dying process,
drained of emotion and ability to concentrate,
intense anger at thoughtless words of others,
intense feelings of loss of normal routines,
an emptiness in their lives,
a large gap where their loved one was,
the physical presence missing, familiar smells gone,
the emotional support no longer there.

No right to enjoy a sunny day,
guilt at the first laughs and jokes
or moments of thinking of other things,
I have no right to happiness
with my loved one no longer here.

Grief will ebb and flow,
waves coming, then receding as with the ocean,
stay with us, yet change.
Gradually the pleasant memories of past days
replace the trauma of our loved one's end,
in time developing strengths not previously known.

Residents and their Possessions

A resident with the most decorated room
with her twenty clocks ticking,
left her room only for mealtime,
rarely interacting with others.

Another resident knew
she had left her former life behind,
was willing to part with most of her possessions.
She knew the loneliness of living alone for years,
no longer able to freely get out to socialize with others,
appreciated the stimulation and company
of others she lived with at the nursing home.

Reflections on War

Outsourcing Actions on Beliefs

Would wars
have the human power
to start and continue on,
if those making the decisions
were to take the
initial steps
at the front of the line?

Would the strongest advocates
of the death penalty
continue on,
if they had to take on
year long duty
in the role of executioner

Living with Fears

from a story on CBC radio and from the Gregory Clark book "Barr'l of Apples"

A woman whose boat capsized
in the middle of a lake
floated alone in a life jacket,
realized by calling help over and over
just made her panic,
so decided to sing every song in her memory,
while calming and soothing her,
voice training she got,
until others heard her and
came to her rescue.

Gregory Clark was a real scaredy cat,
but when stuck in a stuck in a trench
with his football hero,
gunfire and bombs flying overhead,
he talked about all his hero's moves
in his favorite games.
The football hero, when danger had passed,
exclaimed *"Good God, weren't you scared!"*

Gregory replied:
*"I've been scared all my life,
the best thing to do is keep talking
all the way through."*

We are all Jews Here ...

inspired by a story – Discovering Dad by Chris Edmonds, Guideposts Magazine

*W*e are all Jews here, we are all gay,
all are women or bi or transsexual
or of a color, religion or nationality that is despised and blamed.
Are we willing to step forward,
to be the target
of one man's hate,
when he wants to segregate
who he wants to kill
and who can remain?

A grandfather who never
spoke of his POW experiences in the last days of WWII,
of his courageous stand at Zeigenhain,
as officer Roddie Edmonds
instructed all his men to disobey
when they asked for all Jews to step forward,
in unison made the move,
declaring *we are all Jews here.*

In Canada we had
Marc Lepine target women
studying to be engineers,
native women and men
have been murdered in high numbers.
black people killed in all circumstance by those hired to protect,
In Orlando, gays were the chosen target,
followed by members of the police force.
Imagine for a minute,
if we put ourselves in others place
and were as willing as Roddie Edmonds
to declare
what you plan to do to them,
count me in too.

Experiences that become Ours

*I*f we fail to get angry
when an injustice happens,
our country is not a democracy
for all its inhabitants,
we think it only happens to others
not to us.

Someday *we become the others*
to whom it happens.

War's Aftereffects

among Nursing Home residents

May Day, May Day,

Agnes
repeatedly called out,
reliving her past days,
needing to put on a brave face
for her kindergarten students
during the 1940's London's Blitz.

Elkie who lived in
Dresden, Germany's most bombed city,
close to war's end,
rushing to bomb shelters
with her two-year-old in hand,
refused to sleep in a closed room.

Mary
hated the sound of airplanes,
knowing
they changed the capacity of war,
having lost her son
as a pilot in WWII.

Giselle,
knew the war had changed her husband,
returning from all the horrors,
turned to drinking, violent at times
the beatings she endured following,
secrets needed telling.

No Way to Win at War

inspired by a story in Nelly McClung's biography by a family member

$\mathcal{J}$ack, oldest son of Nelly and Wes McClung,
went to war a teenage boy, returned an old man,
the weight of the world on his shoulders,
the sights, sounds,
taste, smell and touch of war,
an unending burden on his soul.

A stranger came up to him, gave a pat on the back,
asked: *how does it feel to win a war?*
Jack replied, I *did not know that wars were ever won!*
If they are, it's certainly not by the people who do the fighting.

War spreads the seeds of future animosity,
grudges and simmering resentment
of those who inflicted such pain on so many families.

For the victors, who lost many buddies at war,
scenes of carnage both from the enemy and their own inflicted,
cities, communities, homes, nature, sence of security forever changed,
the awareness of how easy it is to get caught up in war's brutality,
the trauma of horrors burned into one's mind,
altering their ability to relate to others in peacetime,
disabilities and addictions affect generations behind.

Drugs and Alcohol – Wars' Fuel

An assumption made,
addictions of drug and alcohol abuse,
the after effects of many wars,
a way to try to forget
realities they lived through,
of people injured and killed,
communities destroyed
the people they were able to help,
those they have injured more,
buddies injured and killed,
trauma after trauma, attempted to be buried again and again.

Yet Hitler is now known
to have taken eighty pills a day,
many soldiers were able
to keep fighting with daily supplies of uppers,
feeding their *bravery and stamina,*
child soldiers often initiated
by given drugs to deaden their emotions
in order to fulfill their killing duties,
given from their Generals.

Drugs and alcohol utilized
to forget to feel,
emotions tied to being fully human,
reactions to what they are doing.

The Value in an offer to See a Movie

inspired by the actions of Heinrich Steinmeyer, three teenage girls of Comrie, Scotland
first told to "As it Happens" CBC radio

*I*f willing to cross lines drawn in war
between the enemy and the occupied,
depends on the label
you want to stick on a man,
as it alters your attitude and actions.
SS officer, Nazi, the enemy,
or a nineteen-year old man,
behind a withholding fence,
the captured enemy
given a momentary chance of escape
from confining roles,
an ability to imagine something different.

Never before did he have a chance
to see a moving picture, the thrill of his lifetime,
when three teenage girls
helped him have an escape,
borrowing one brothers's school uniform,
he was ordered to stay quiet,
as they went together as a group to the movies,
later brought back to the camp.

After the war,
he stayed in Scotland for twenty-five years,
his attachment so deep,
he wanted his ashes scattered
on the hills surrounding the town of Comrie.
When he left this earth,
he left his life savings to the town people,
a sign of unending gratitude.

Artistic Expressions that Save

based on a Toronto Star story by Louise Brown

My people will sleep for one hundred years,
but when they awaken, it will be the artists
who will give them their spirits back.

What Louis Riel captured in this quote,
Alice Herz-Sommer lived.
One hundred and ten years she thrived,
since the age of five
playing piano,
her devotion to music kept her alive.

While in Terezin,
later Auschwitz
she lost her mother and husband,
still was able to play,
adding laughter, joy:
her music, food,
her tunes, medicine,
melodies added hope,
nourishing many.

As the oldest survivor of the death camps,
she stated:
We are all the same, both good and bad.
Alice in her life
showed there can be another way,
living creatively each day.

Clothespins Connections

from a PBS documentary – Children of Syria

*T*he same multi-colored plastic clothespins I use,
the mother used
going about her weekly laundry tasks,
attempts at life's normality,
in uncommon times.
Sheets hung across in alley ways
and streets,
a way to block a sniper's vision
of targets he sought.

For so long they tried to carry on,
the father, an engineer, turned rebel leader
against the oppressive, violent, Syrian regime.
Four children in the family,
he took on the fight for Syria's future, for what is right,
hoping the daily bombings and weaponry
would not hit them on the spot.

The young girls scavenging through
empty neighbourhood ghost like abandoned homes,
arguing against older siblings and parental authority:
why can't we keep their abandoned toys?
"It isn't right – they just might return".
Play acting at what they see,
pretending to be the enemy,
trying to process all their fears and life's uncertainties.

The father taken away from his office by ISIS one day,
rumors of a horrible beating,
ever-remaining questions: did he survive?

How horrible it is, when people sharing your religion in name,
not in their hate-inspired violent practices.

Finally a decision to leave,
an opening has occurred
to migrate to Germany,
a process by van, short stay in a muddy tent refugee camp,
then a first ever flight by plane.

Welcomed into a small town,
with an aging population,
the children adapt in making friends.
In time, some rumblings of resentment
against *those refugees*,
lingering feelings of
disconnection from their roots in Syria,
language, relatives, culture.

The Mother in the family
sacrificed all in this move to Germany
to focus on her children's future well-being,
regularly sent pictures
of men horribly abused who died,
trying to determine: *is this my husband?*
has the most difficulty in adapting,
lingering depression and grief uncertain,
less opportunities for socialization
and connection.

Refugees are coming to a different life,
much safer for sure,
not all in their new country will be better,
as they have lost so much connections
to who they really are.

The Best Cook in the World

dedicated to George Emerson and Henk Metselaar,
from a Toronto Star story by Alex Ballingall

A young man worked to near starvation in the German labour camps,
where my grandfather also was held,
following the war, a skeleton barely able to make his way home.

A Canadian serviceman cooked and fed him
a meal of potatoes and bully beef, to great satisfaction.
Yet knowing he would need more to carry him his journey through,
remembered the two chocolate bars his parents had sent,
decided to give this to provide energy to keep him walking.

The young man recovered, remembered the generosity,
immigrated to Canada in time,
always having in the back of his mind,
someday he would meet his gentle benefactor so kind.

A chance meeting for the soldier in a furniture store,
with the daughter of this labour camp survivor,
one of a family of six children that came to be,
because of a soldier's generosity.

The long awaited reunion came at last,
the camp survivor with Alzheimers,
asked when he left *where did that man go?*

LaShay's Memorable Hug

from a Toronto Star story by Robin Levinson King

*A*fter years of working in Afghanistan, New Orleans and the Philipines,
a US air force pararescuer, Michael Maroney's
dark images of massive deaths and destruction
lingered on in his mind.

The thing that sustained him
through many dark times
was the memory of a three-year-old's smile and a hug
from Hurricane Katrina's worst days.

LaShay Brown, rescued with her mother,
a week without food and water,
even now ten years later,
the family struggles on
with low pay in Mississipi.

Yet in her own way
LaShay turned the tables,
gave strength to Michael her rescuer,
into his retirement days.

A reunion arranged
by a friend of his son,
was the best ever retirement present
one could have.

Wartime Connections

from 101, Airborne Museum, Bastogne, Big Geek Daddy videos

$\mathcal{J}$ack Leroy Tueller, two weeks after D-day
was miserable and stressed
on a dark rainy night, mud-filled trench,
he pulled out his trumpet,
told by his commander
you can't play it now, there's still a sniper out there.

He knew this lonely sniper across enemy lines,
probably felt the same way,
decided to connect with him
by playing a German love song:
Underneath the lantern ... my own Lili Marlene ...

The next day a jeep came with German prisoners
from further down the beach,
one insisting he wanted to know
who played the trumpet the night before,
when introduced, the two shook hands,
he explained how the music
made him think of his fiance, parents and siblings,
how it stopped him from firing,
to put an end to this expression of hate,
choosing to focus on love instead.

———————

Vince Speranza
fought in the Battle of the Bulge,
was in a town surrounded by enemy lines,
the wounded were many and placed in the Church,
he went to find and comfort his wounded friend
who asked for a beer he desperately craved.

The first bar was too damaged,
but the second he found
had beer on tap, a container he must find,
as his helmet was handy,
he filled it to the brim
returned to quench his buddy's thirst,
only to find many others had the same need.
He returned many times with his helmet of beer
to meet many needs, to aid and give comfort to the wounded,
until discovered by the Major Surgeon who put a stop to this practice.
Sixty-five years later, he returned with his daughter to the site,
after finding his foxhole, remembering the night,
when enemy soldiers caught in barbed wire in the snow,
how snow turned red in his first combat role,
later trying to erase the images,
he shared wine with war buddies,
then in time shared about serving beer in his helmet.
The buddies couldn't believe that this new companion
was the source of a local legend,
then asked the bartender to bring some *Airborne Beer,*
bottles with a picture of a para-trooper serving beer in a helmet,
the beer was to be poured into a mini china helmet.

Just two WWII soldiers,
who didn't do as they were told,
acting independently
to make a difference
in saving lives,
instilling hope and connections
in unusual ways.

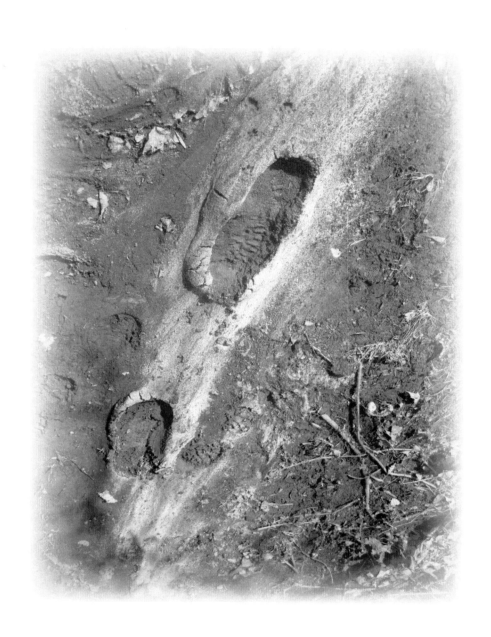

Poetry in the Mud of Life

inspired by a story by Katie Daubs in the Toronto Star

Canon Frederick Scott, a Padre
who tread along side
his soldiers
in trenches of mud,
no place
considered too dangerous
for him to walk in.

In days of misery,
boredom
and fear,
he came by
to dispense cigarettes, candy
and in daily doses recited his poetry.

Words to delight in nature,
encourage in everyday struggles,
work through the emotions
of living the realities of fighting a war.

Our lives no longer
in these trenches,
yet still in great need,
of daily doses of poetry.